A N

DK READERS is a compelling reading children. The programme is designed i leading literacy experts, including Cliff Moon M.Ed., who has spent many years as a teacher and teacher educator specializing in reading. Cliff Moon has written more than 160 books for children and teachers. He is series editor to Collins Big Cat.

Beautiful illustrations and superb full-colour photographs combine with engaging, easy-to-read stories to offer a fresh approach to each subject in the series. Each DK READER is guaranteed to capture a child's interest while developing his or her reading skills, general knowledge, and love of reading.

The five levels of DK READERS are aimed at different reading abilities, enabling you to choose the books that are exactly right for your child:

Pre-level 1: Learning to read
Level 1: Beginning to read
Level 2: Beginning to read alone
Level 3: Reading alone
Level 4: Proficient readers

The "normal" age at which a child begins to read can be anywhere from three to eight years old. Adult participation through the lower levels is very helpful for providing encouragement, discussing storylines and sounding out unfamiliar words.

1 6 SEP 2011

No matter which level you select, you can be sure that you are helping your child learn to read, then read to learn!

LONDON, NEW YORK, MUNICH,
MELBOURNE, AND DELHI

Series Editor Deborah Lock
Senior Art Editor Tory Gordon-Harris
Design Assistant Sadie Thomas
Production Editor Sean Daly
Jacket Designer Natalie Godwin
Publishing Manager Bridget Giles

Reading Consultant
Cliff Moon, M.Ed.

Published in Great Britain by
Dorling Kindersley Limited
80 Strand, London WC2R 0RL

A CIP catalogue record for this book
is available from the British Library

ISBN: 978-1-40535-345-8

Colour reproduction by Colourscan, Singapore
Printed and bound in China by L. Rex Printing Co. Ltd.

The publisher would like to thank the following for their kind
permission to reproduce their photographs:
a=above; c=centre; b=below; l=left; r=right t=top;

Ardea London Ltd: 23tr; **Corbis:** Wolfgang Kaehler 13c. Rob C.
Nunnington/Gallo Images 28tl; **Philip Dowell:** 26-27; **Getty Images:**
Arthur S.Aubry 30-31; Geoff du Feu 10tl; David McGlynn 4cl; Laurence
Monneret 31c; Tom Schierlitz 27br; Bob Stefko 18l; Kevin Summers
20-21; **Natural History Museum:** 2cra, 7cbr, 24bl, 24br, 25bl, 25bc,
25bcr, 32tl, 32bl; **N.H.P.A:** Stephen Dalton 15tr; David Middleton
4-5; **Oxford Scientific Film:** 8tl, 8-9, 9tc, Claude Steelman/SAL 6-7;
Jerry Young: 11bc, 26bl;
Jacket images: _Front:_ **Alamy Images:** D. Hurst

All other images © Dorling Kindersley
For further imformation see: www.dkimages.com
</td>

Discover more at
www.dk.com

Garden Friends

A Dorling Kindersley Book

butterfly

garden

Meet the small animals
in my garden.

nail

antenna

flower

butterflies

Hello, butterfly.
You are resting
on a flower.

———wing

leaf

eye

mouth

 caterpillars

Hello, caterpillar.
You are eating
a big leaf.

spot

 ladybirds

Hello, ladybirds.
How many spots
do you have?

head

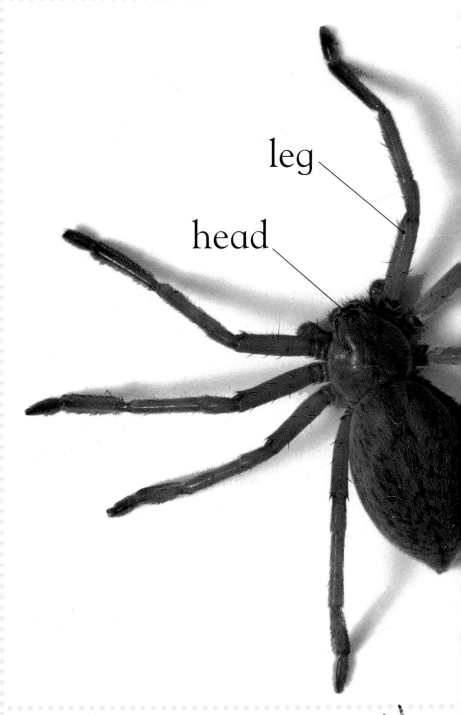

leg

head

 spiders

Hello, spider.
You have spun
a big web.

eb

flower

furry body

 bumblebees

Hello, bumblebee.
You are drinking
from a flower.

Hello, centipede.
How many legs
do you have?

centipedes

head

leg

Hello, dragonfly.
You are flying
around very fast.

 dragonflies

wing

leg

19

baby snail

shell

snails

Hello, snail.
You have a baby
on your back.

soft body

worms

Hello, worms.
Which one is
the longest?

Hello, stag beetle.
You have very
sharp jaws.

wing

jaw

ead

Hello, frogs.
You are hiding
in the grass.

foot

frogs

grasshoppers

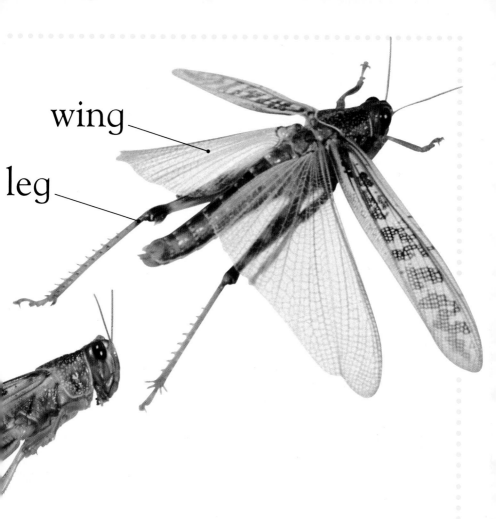

wing

leg

Hello, grasshoppers.
Wow!
What a big jump!

dragonfly

 Which animals are

in your garden?

Glossary

Antennae are used by insects to feel their surroundings

Centipede an insect with many legs

Jaws are used by stag beetles to fight and nip

Shell the hard outside covering on some animals

Web some spiders make webs to catch prey, and as a place to rest